RENEWING
Your Mind

Transformation is a life long process

VELYN COOPER

ISBN: 978-1-4669-0877-2 (sc)
ISBN: 978-1-4669-0878-9 (e)

Trafford rev. 01/16/2012

 www.trafford.com

North America & international
toll-free: 1 888 232 4444 (USA & Canada)
phone: 250 383 6864 ♦ fax: 812 355 4082

Contents

Introduction

THE BIGGEST PROBLEM for some of us is the way we see ourselves because what we see on the inside, is what we become on the outside. Our minds need to be renewed according to the Word of God, so that we can see things the way that He wants us to see it and become the persons that He created us to be.

Romans 12:2 says, And be not conformed to this world: but be ye transformed by the renewing of your mind, that ye may prove what is that good, acceptable and perfect will of God.

To conform means to adapt to your surroundings. In other words you accept whatever circumstance, situation or location you are in as normal and do absolutely nothing to change it. This is a very dangerous position for Christians to be in because when we conform to the standards of the world, it sends out a mixed message to the unsaved, that it is all right to be a child of God and still be a part of the lifestyle of the world.

The word transform has the opposite meaning of the word conform. While the person who conforms adapts to his or her surroundings, the person who transforms makes a difference in his or her surroundings.

As Christians, we are living in the world, but our attitudes and actions must be different from the people who have not accepted Jesus Christ as their personal Lord and Saviour. We need to be transformed or changed from the way we used to be, to the way we are to be in Christ,

Velyn Cooper

according to the Word of God, The Bible. This transformation can only take place, if we become actively involved in the process, by diligently studying the Word of God, allowing the Holy Spirit to give us understanding of the Word and then making every effort to apply the Word in our lives.

1) What does it mean to conform to your surroundings?

_____
_____
_____

2) What does it mean to transform your surroundings?

_____
_____
_____

Chapter One

SEED OF DESIRE

The Mind

THE MIND IS that part of us that makes us aware of who we are, what we are and where we are. Through it we think, feel, make choices, have desires, collect memories and discover both our purpose and the tools necessary to accomplish our purpose. It is the seat of our consciousness. It is the most fertile soil that God has ever created. It is so fruitful and rich that whatever seed of desire you plant in it—whether good or bad—will reproduce in great abundance.

David had a seed of desire to build a temple for the Lord but because of the many people he killed during times of war, God told him he wouldn't be allowed to do it. His son Solomon would build the temple instead. Solomon had not even been born when God told this to David, but the seed of desire was already planted in David's mind. He had a vision of how he wanted the temple to look and what kind of materials he wanted to use for the building. This building had to be the best.

When Solomon was just a young boy, David began making provisions for the construction of the temple. He provided gold, silver, brass and iron in abundance. He even provided the wood and stone. To top it off, when Solomon was old enough to start building the temple, he didn't even have to look for skilled laborers—David already had them in place. He even gave Solomon the plan he was to follow when building the temple, to be certain that it was built or reproduced according to what he saw in his mind.

David's seed of desire gave him a clear picture of what would be manifested in reality, through a son who had not yet been born. This caused him to take the necessary steps in providing what would be needed to bring his seed of desire to pass—down to the very last detail. His seed of desire was passed on to his son, along with the physical and financial means necessary to bring it to pass.

It took seven years to build the temple. David knew that he would not be alive during the time that it was being built, but his seed of desire was so strong, that the vision was caught by his son, who not only shared it and did all he could to fulfill it, but made his father's vision a part of his own (1 Chronicles 22).

Even though David knew that he would not be around for the complete fulfillment of his seed of desire, he nurtured it, developed it and made all of the necessary arrangements to have it brought to fruition. He wasn't concerned about who would get the credit for his idea, He was concerned about a house being built for God, where all of the people could come and worship and give thanks for His many blessings toward them.

What seed of desire do you have and what are you doing about it? Are you cultivating, nurturing and developing it or are you ignoring it because you think it is out of your league? Or, maybe you're being selfish, because you know that you will not be around long enough for its complete fulfillment and you don't want anyone else getting credit for your work!

If you are not fulfilling your seed of desire, what are you doing about it? Is it lying dormant in the recesses of your mind, locked in by all of the cares and anxieties of life? Are you afraid of it or are you just too lazy to apply the necessary effort to bring it to fruition?

If money is the problem and God gave you the vision, He will provide the means necessary for you to get the money that you need to fulfill the vision. Whatever the reason search through all of the dust and cobwebs of your mind, find your seed of desire and begin work on its development today. You will be amazed at the new outlook you will have on life and the sense of purpose and direction that will begin to dominate your mind.

REVIEW

1) Explain the workings of the mind.

_____
_____
_____
_____
_____
_____

2) Why was David not allowed to build the temple?

_____
_____
_____
_____
_____
_____

3) Who would be the one to build the temple?

_____

4) Was this person born when God instructed David about the building of the temple?

_____

5) When did David start making preparations for the building of the temple?

_____

_____
_____
_____
_____
_____

6) What preparations did David make for the building of the temple?

_____
_____
_____
_____
_____

7) What did David's seed of desire do for him?

_____
_____
_____
_____

8) How long did it take to build the temple?

_____
_____

9) What caused David's son to catch the vision to build the temple?

_____
_____
_____
_____
_____

10) Was David's concern regarding the building of the temple one of
   selfishness? Why? Why not?

_____

_____

_____

_____

_____

_____

Chapter Two

A WILLING MIND

David

DAVID HAD A willing mind to be used of God in any capacity God chose. So, when God told him that he would not be allowed to build the temple, he didn't get upset and have a bad attitude toward God or Solomon, whom God had chosen to build the temple. He was committed to the vision of building the temple and it didn't matter to him if God used someone else to fulfill it. His willing mind gave him the determination he needed to make all the necessary provisions for the fulfillment of the vision—even to the minutest detail. He was operating in willing obedience to God.

On the other hand we are not so much like that today. Imagine that you are working for a large corporation and you come up with an idea that will mean a lot of money for the corporation and probably even a promotion for you. You gather all of your information, make a presentation to your bosses and they love it. You're not even wondering who will be allowed to execute the idea. You came up with it and as far as you are concerned, no one else but you will be the one to bring it to fruition. You start spending money you don't have and celebrating even before the victory is won.

Unfortunately, the bosses have another idea. They feel that another employee would be more successful in bringing the idea to life and give the project to them. You are asked to assist your co-worker in any way necessary to ensure the success of the project. What would be your response to your bosses and your reaction to your co-worker? Do you think you would be able to continue working with him or her comfortably and willingly or would you quit and look for another job?

That's a tough one, but we have the same Spirit of God that David had, so we too can support the ministry like he did.

Joseph and Mary

Joseph and Mary were engaged to be married, when she became pregnant—but not by him. In spite of this, Joseph, being a gentleman, didn't want her to be embarrassed in any way. He decided to leave her quietly, but the angel of God stopped him. He came to Joseph in a dream explaining to him that for the purpose of the salvation of mankind, Mary was impregnated through the Holy Spirit.

Matthew 1: 18-21(NIV)

18) This is how the birth of Jesus Christ came about: His mother Mary, was pledged to be married to Joseph, but before they came together, she was found to be with child through the Holy Spirit

19) Because Joseph her husband (*fiancée*) was a righteous man and did not want to expose her to public disgrace, he had in mind to divorce her quietly. (*break off the engagement*)

20) But after he had considered this, an angel of the Lord appeared to him in a dream and said "Joseph son of David, do not be afraid to take Mary home as your wife, because what is conceived in her is from the Holy Spirit.

21) She will give birth to a son, and you are to give him the name Jesus, because He will save His people from their sins".

Joseph could have said no to marrying Mary after finding out that she was pregnant and he was not the father. We would have understood, because there are very few men if any, who would continue with their wedding plans once they found out that their fiancée was pregnant by someone else—even if the someone else was of divine origin! Joseph made a conscious choice to become Mary's husband. He had a willing mind to live in obedience to God.

1) What was David's attitude and commitment to the vision when God told him he would not be allowed to build the temple?

_____

_____

_____

_____

_____

_____

2) Would you be able to go ahead with your marriage plans if you discovered that your fiancé got another woman pregnant or your fiancée was pregnant for another man? Why? Why not?

_____

_____

_____

_____

_____

_____

_____

Daniel

Daniel was born in Jerusalem. He was a young man when Nebuchadnezzar, King of Babylon, attacked his city, took control and carried him, along with many other of his countrymen to Babylon, to live and work at whatever jobs they were assigned to. Because of his good looks, academic and athletic abilities, he was one of the chosen few who were selected to be trained to work in the king's palace. (Daniel 1)

Daniel was committed to God wherever he was and was always obedient to His will. As a result of this, he found favor with God and favor with man. He was placed in positions of authority under the rule of Nebuchadnezzar and under the rule of Nebuchadnezzar's son, Belshazzar, but the favor didn't stop there. No matter who was in charge, he found favor with them because he lived his life in obedience to God.

Darius the Mede overthrew Babylon, killed Belshazzar and became King. He appointed one hundred and twenty princes over the kingdom, with three presidents in authority over them. Daniel, still walking in the favor of God, was not only selected to be one of the presidents—he was also put in charge of the other two presidents.

He was preferred over the other presidents because there was an excellent spirit in him. The King put him in charge of everything and everyone. Of course the other two presidents and the princes didn't like this. They got to work trying to find a way to discredit him. They looked high and low, up and down and all around to find some way of discrediting Daniel, but they could find none. They decided that the only way they would be able to catch him in any kind of trap would be through his commitment to the laws of God.

They convinced the King to create a new law saying that if anyone prayed to any god or man, except the King, within thirty days, they would be thrown into a den of lions. Once the law was put into effect, the presidents and the princes waited eagerly to see what Daniel would do. Daniel respected the authority of the King but his obligations and commitment were to Almighty God first. He was willing only to be in total submission and obedience to his God, the one true God and no price was too high to pay for that obedience.

Before the King created the new law, Daniel was a man who spent time with God in prayer three times a day, every day. It was never something he did in secret. He always opened his windows, which were facing

Jerusalem, and knelt down and prayed to God publicly. After the law went into effect, he continued to pray as he always did. No law of man would ever over-ride his willingness to acknowledge and worship God and God alone. The other presidents and princes saw to it that the King honoured his law and against the King's desire, Daniel was thrown into the lions den. The King, convinced by Daniel's commitment to God, had faith that God would deliver Daniel. His words to Daniel were: "Thy God whom thou servest continually, He will deliver thee."

The King couldn't sleep at all that night and first thing the next morning, he ran to the lion's den to see if Daniel was all right. Daniel was fine because he was protected by God. The men who set him up to be thrown into the lion's den were thrown in themselves and needless to say, they were not as fortunate as Daniel and the lions tore them to shreds. (Daniel 6)

Imagine that we were in Daniel's position and our life depended on whether we honored our commitment to man over our commitment to God. Can we really imagine what might go through some of our minds and how difficult it would be for some of us to make that decision?

Some people might say that for thirty days, Daniel could have prayed in secret because God hears our prayer no matter where we are. That is all well and good, but once you have already established a mode of operation and you have already taken a bold step in worshipping God publicly, no matter where you may be living, what is it saying to the general public when a decree, such as the one made by the King is given and you honor the King or your governmental leader instead of God?

Do you think that Daniel would have continued being a good witness for God if he had submitted to the King's decree? Definitely not!

When the King made the decree that prayers or petitions were to be made only to him, he set himself up as God, the Creator and Supplier of all that is and he was not that.

Daniel's decision to continue with his times of prayer as normal was more than a ritual and more than being disobedient to the King. He had a choice to make as to whom he would serve as God. He was not willing to jeopardize his relationship with God in any way nor was he willing to influence his people in a negative way regarding their relationship with God. If he had discontinued his times of public prayer he would have been acknowledging the King as God and the many people who looked to him as an example of a God-fearing man would have been broken spiritually.

Daniel had a willing mind to do one thing and one thing only—to bring glory and honor to God by worshipping Him and Him only as God.

Be a Daniel by being a godly example in every situation, no matter what position you may hold or what the cost might be. Why? When all is over and done, it is only what is done for God that truly matters.

Here are some questions to ponder that only you can truly answer for yourself. What are you doing to bring honour and glory to God? How are you taking a stand for Him throughout each day, wherever you may be, regardless of who might be around? Can the people that you live and work with, say that you are truly a child of God because of your attitude and behavior toward them or are they wondering why you are making a fool of yourself by pretending to be a child of God and you're not?

What you are on the inside will definitely be revealed on the outside. You can talk salvation and Bible all you want, but if you are not living salvation and living Bible, be quiet. You are only fooling yourself and being a stumbling block to others and God will deal with you accordingly.

If you are not sure of where you stand in your faith (relationship with God), examine yourself to make sure that you are on the right track with Him. If you aren't on the right track, trust me, the people around you know by your actions.

2ⁿᵈ Corinthians 13:5 (NIV)

Examine yourself to see whether you are in the faith; test your selves. Do you not realize that Jesus Christ is in you—unless, of course, you fail the test?

You have to examine yourself according to the word of God to see whether or not you are living in accordance to the will of God. Be honest with yourself. You are the only person who knows who you really are and what you really are about—what you think about yourself and others, how you feel about yourself and others and whether or not you are pretending to be something that you are not.

You may get away with the pretense while you are on earth, but trust me, one day you will have to give an account of your life to God who knows everything and you cannot pretend with Him. He will reward you according to the life that you have lived and He will reward you according to the truth of His Word.

Galatians 6:7

Be not deceived; God is not mocked: for whatever a man soweth, that shall he also reap.

Every human being on this earth is a farmer and we are all sowing some type of seed every day of our lives. Whatever seed we sow has an eternal effect on our souls.

If you are a child of God and you are living according to His word, you are sowing seeds of righteousness in good fertile soil, which will bring you rewards in this life and in the life to come.

If you are not a child of God, whatever seeds you are sowing are being sown in barren ground or bad soil. Even though you may see a few benefits while you are on earth, these benefits will not survive in this life and they will definitely not carry over into the next life. You will discover that all of your efforts in this life were in vain.

Don't be afraid to be honest with yourself about who you really are— that is the beginning of farming in good soil and that is what the enemy is trying to stop you from doing. The enemy doesn't want you to start farming in the good fertile soil because the enemy knows that is the first step in truly coming to terms with where you are or are not in Christ. Once you can accept the truth of the Word of God and the truth about yourself, the enemy will no longer have a hold on your life, because the truth makes us free.

John 8:28 (Jesus is speaking)

And ye shall know the truth, and the truth shall make you free.

Accept the truth about yourself—the good the bad and the ugly. Present them all to God. Allow Him to put everything in perspective for you and to guide you into His truth. Once you allow Him to do this, your mind will begin to be renewed according to His word; you will begin to grow in the things of God; you will begin to realize the potential that God has given you; you will begin to walk in the purpose for which He has created you and in the fullness of the blessings that He has in store for you.

REVIEW

1) Where was Daniel born?

_____

2) How did he get to Babylon?

_____
_____
_____
_____

3) Why was he chosen to work in the palace of the king of Babylon?

_____
_____
_____
_____

4) Why did Daniel have favor with God?

_____
_____
_____
_____

5) Who took over the leadership of Babylon after the death of Nebuchadnezzar?

_____

6) Who overthrew Babylon and killed the new king?

_____

7) Why was Daniel preferred over the other presidents?

_____
_____
_____
_____

8) What did Daniel do three times a day?

_____

9) What did the other presidents do as a result of Daniel's favor with the king?

_____
_____
_____
_____

10) What was the new law that the other presidents convinced the king to create in order to cause problems for Daniel?

_____
_____
_____
_____
_____
_____

11) Did Daniel change his lifestyle after the new law was created?

_____

12) What was the result of what he did?

_____

_____

13) Explain the importance of Daniel's decision to continue with his times of prayer.

_____

_____

_____

_____

14) When it comes to our relationship with God, who should we examine? Why?

_____

_____

_____

_____

15) According to Galatians 6: 7, what do we reap?

_____

_____

Our respect for the authority of the land should not interfere with our obligation and commitment to God.

Chapter Three

AN UNWILLING MIND

Jonah

JONAH WAS A man of God who at one point, experienced a bout with an unwilling mind. God sent him to the city of Nineveh to cry against it—to speak against the wrong they were doing. The city would be over thrown because of the wickedness of the people. Jonah didn't want to go and instead, caught a boat going in the opposite direction. The boat was caught in a raging storm, with everyone panicking and fearing for their lives—everyone except Jonah. He slept through the whole ordeal. When it was determined that he was the cause of the angry seas, it was decided and agreed upon by all on board—including Jonah—that he be thrown overboard. He was and the sea was immediately calmed. (Jonah 1)

God made provision for a big fish to swallow Jonah and vomit him up on dry land, after three days of being in its belly. (Jonah 2:10)

God again told Jonah to deliver the message he sent him to preach and this time he did. All of the people believed—rich and poor. The King left the throne, took of his robe, wore sackcloth and sat in ashes. (This is a sign of mourning). The people and the animals also wore sackcloth. The King commanded that no food be eaten and there was to be no drinking of anything—not even water—by any person or animal. Everyone was to cry out to God and stop doing whatever they were doing that was wrong, in the hope that God would forgive them. God saw the sincerity of their actions, forgave them and decided against having the city over thrown. (Jonah 3)

This positive turn of events should have filled Jonah with joy. He should have been ecstatic to know that the people received the message he delivered from God and turned from doing the wrong they had become accustomed to. On top of that, their lives were spared. Instead, he was angry that God didn't wipe them out.

Jonah showed unwillingness to be obedient to God in two ways. He was unwilling to go to Nineveh and deliver the message God gave him for the people of that city and decided to go elsewhere. God intercepted his plans and got him there anyway. Once he delivered the message and the people repented, he was unwilling for God to forgive them and show them mercy, by sparing them the destruction He had intended for them.

Are you like Jonah? If he had his way, he would have allowed the destruction of everything and everyone in Nineveh, without a second thought and he would have become a force to reckon with. In his mind and in the mind of anyone else who heard about what had happened, he would have become someone to whom great respect and admiration was given. He would have become like a god to those who didn't know any better because they, like him, would have believed that the destruction of Nineveh was by his power and not the power of God.

When God saw the sincerity in the repentance of the people, being the righteous God that He is, He chose to forgive them. Jonah, being the selfish man that he was, didn't care about the salvation of the people, he only cared about how he would look to the people after God forgave them and spared their lives. He should have been grateful that God chose him as a vessel of honor, worthy to be used in such a powerful deliverance ministry. Instead of being angry at God for being merciful, he should have been thanking God for the privilege of being a part of such an awesome demonstration of the rewards of true repentance.

Are you delivering the Word of God in the power and authority granted to you by Him, then when people turn from their sins and choose to be obedient to Him, you are disappointed? Why? Your job is ended and you will no longer get the respect from them that made you feel like you were superior to them!

What about when you're in church and it's time for the altar call? Have you noticed how some Pastors take the altar call personally and if no one responds to the call of salvation, they become offended, as it were something against them? To satisfy themselves, they would run down a list of every possible situation, asking people to come. If you're sick, come. If you're in debt, come. If you're having marital problems, come—and the list goes on and on and on. They will not stop until someone comes to that altar for prayer. They act as if it is their own personal altar call and they are promoted or demoted by the amount of people that respond to it.

All born again Christians have a responsibility to spread the word of God. We don't have to be the Pastor of a church or have any position whatsoever in the church. As children of God, we are all responsible for sharing the word of God, especially with those who have not yet accepted God's way of life. It is not about us, it is all about bringing glory to God, our Creator and Saviour.

We have the responsibility of sharing the word with others, but God uses us how He chooses in getting His word delivered. He uses some to plant the seed of His word and He uses some to water those seeds, but the actual increase in the life giving properties of those seeds come from Him and Him alone.

During the time of the ministries of Paul and Apollos, they were faced with the problem of people who accepted the message of Jesus Christ through their ministry, claiming them as their deliverers. As far as the people were concerned they belonged either to Paul or they belonged to Apollos. Paul had to explain to them that he and Apollos were only being used by God to bring forth His word and any change in their lives was brought about by the power of God and not by them.

The people didn't belong to Paul or to Apollos—they belonged to God.

1 Corinthians 3: 4-7 (NIV) Paul says,

4) For when one says, "I follow Paul," and another, I follow Apollos, "Are you not mere Men?

5) What, after all, is Apollos? And what is Paul? Only servants, through whom you came to believe—as the Lord has assigned to each his task

6) I planted the seed; Apollos watered it, but God made it grow.

7) So neither he who plants nor he who waters is anything, but only God who makes things grow.

For Jonah it was all about Jonah. He was concerned about how he would look in the eyes of the people after God saw their humility, heard their confession, forgave their sins and delivered them. That was more important to him than the salvation of their souls.

Don't be a Jonah. Ask the Lord to give you the courage to go where He sends you, preach the message He gives you and the wisdom to rejoice when the non—believers hear and accept His word.

REVIEW

1) Why was God going to overthrow the city of Nineveh?

_____
_____
_____
_____
_____
_____
_____
_____

2) What was the result of Jonah's disobedience?

_____
_____
_____
_____

3) How did God save Jonah from the raging sea?

_____
_____
_____
_____

4) What happened after Jonah delivered the message to the people of Nineveh?

_____
_____
_____

_____

_____

_____

5) Was Jonah pleased with the response of the people? Why? Why not?

_____

_____

_____

_____

_____

_____

6) In which two ways did Jonah show unwillingness to be obedient to God?

_____

_____

_____

_____

_____

_____

_____

_____

7) When God saw the sincerity in the repentance of the people of Nineveh, what did He do?

_____

_____

8) What is the responsibility of all born again Christians?

_____

_____

_____

_____

Velyn Cooper

9) What is a sign or symbol of mourning?

_____

_____

10) According to 1st Corinthians 3: 4-7, what is the process of spiritual growth?

_____

_____

_____

_____

Chapter Four

A FOOLISH MIND

A FOOLISH MIND DOES not belong to a person who is mentally challenged—it belongs to a person who is quite capable of functioning independently in society, but acts without judgment. In other words, it belongs to a person who acts before they think. Hezekiah was such a man.

<u>Hezekiah</u>

Hezekiah was the twelfth king of Judah. He reigned for 29 years. During the first few years of his reign, he did what was right in the sight of the Lord. He cleansed the temple of all the impurities his father had allowed, repaired and reopened the temple and destroyed any sign of idol worship, which was encouraged by his father. He trusted in the Lord so much that he was described as a King who had no other King before or after his rule, who was like him. He was obedient to the Lord in all things. As a result, God was with him and caused him to prosper wherever he went.

Four years into Hezekiah's reign, Israel was attacked by the King of Assyria. It took three years of war, but the King of Assyria was successful in capturing Israel. The people of Israel were deported from Samaria to Assyria. God allowed this to happen because the people of Israel had stopped obeying His commandments.

Fourteen years into Hezekiah's reign, Judah was captured by Assyria. Hezekiah sent a message to the king telling him that if he withdrew from the city of Judah he would pay him whatever he asked for. The King demanded three hundred talents of silver and thirty talents of gold. That was a lot of money, but Hezekiah gave him what he asked for. He gave him all the silver from the temple and the treasuries of the royal palace, including the gold from the doors and doorposts of the temple.

After withdrawing as agreed, the King of Assyria sent an entourage of his officers to Judah with a message for Hezekiah. The message was given to the people, who in turn were to tell Hezekiah to make peace with the King of Assyria. If Hezekiah agreed, the King of Assyria would allow them to stay and live on their property, eat from their own trees and drink from their own wells, until he was ready to take them to Assyria to become his slaves. (2 Kings 18)

When Hezekiah got this bit of news, he put on sackcloth and ashes (a symbol of mourning) and went into the temple. He also made the palace administrator, the secretary and the leading priests wear sackcloth and sent them to see Isaiah the prophet. Isaiah told them to tell Hezekiah that everything would be all right because the Lord would make him victorious over the King of Assyria. As Isaiah said, so it was. (2 Kings 19)

Around that time, Hezekiah became very ill. The Lord sent Isaiah to him to tell him to get his house in order because he was going to die. Hezekiah prayed to the Lord and God healed him and granted him fifteen more years. It was during this time that Hezekiah's mind became foolish. The King of Babylon heard about his illness and sent him some get-well cards along with some presents. Hezekiah got a little carried away by all of this and his excitement got the better part of him. He showed the gift bearers everything that he had—all of the silver and gold, the fine oil, his weapons of war and whatever else he could find for them to see. He left no stone unturned.

Isaiah, God's man of the hour was on top of things as usual. He questioned Hezekiah about the men—where they came from, what they saw and what they said. Hezekiah told Isaiah that the men saw everything and that there was nothing of his treasures that they did not see.

Once Hezekiah confirmed to Isaiah what he had done, Isaiah explained that everything in his palace, including what his forefathers had stored up, would be taken from Judah and given to Babylon—including some of his descendants. (2 Kings 20: 1-18)

What Hezekiah didn't realize was that it is not wise to let your left hand know what your right hand is doing, whether it refers to doing kind deeds for others or displaying all of your wealth and power.

(Matthew 6:3) NIV

(Jesus is speaking) But when you give to the needy, Do not let your left hand know what your right hand is doing.

In other words, don't let people know your business.

Hezekiah felt that God's punishment was good because it would all take place after his death. His response shows that along with having a foolish mind by displaying all of his wealth and weapons to the Babylonians, like Jonah, he too was a selfish man. He could care less about his descendants and the affect his foolish decision would have on them. He was just happy that he wasn't going to be around for any of it. (2 Kings 20: 19-20)

REVIEW

1) To whom does a foolish mind belong?

_____

_____

_____

_____

2) Why did God cause Hezekiah to prosper wherever he went?

_____

_____

_____

_____

3a) When was Israel attacked by the King of Assyria?

_____

_____

3b) How long did it take for Israel to be captured by the King of Assyria?

_____

_____

4) Why did God allow the people of Israel to be captured by the King of Assyria?

_____

_____

_____

_____
_____
_____
_____
_____

5) Where were the people of Israel living when they were captured by the King of Assyria?

_____
_____
_____
_____
_____
_____
_____

6) How long did Hezekiah reign over Judah before Judah was captured by the King of Assyria

_____
_____

7) After Judah was captured by the King of Assyria, what message did the King of Assyria send to Hezekiah?

_____
_____
_____
_____
_____
_____

8) What did Hezekiah do after he received the message from the King of Assyria?

_____
_____
_____
_____
_____
_____

9) What message did the lord give Isaiah for Hezekiah when Hezekiah became ill?

_____
_____
_____
_____
_____
_____
_____
_____

10) What was the mistake that Hezekiah make when the King of Babylon sent get well wishes to him?

_____
_____
_____
_____

11) What did Isaiah tell Hezekiah would be the result of the mistake that he made?

_____
_____

12) Do you believe that along with having a foolish mind, Hezekiah was a selfish man as well?

_____

Chapter 5

A WISE MIND

Joseph

JOSEPH WAS A man with a very wise mind. Pharaoh, the ruler of Egypt had a dream but there was no one on his entire staff who could interpret it for him. In his dream, he was standing by a river and seven fat cows came up out of the river and began to eat grass. Another seven cows came up out of the river and even though these cows were skinny and sick looking, they ate up the seven fat cows. Pharaoh got up and then went back to sleep, only to dream again. In this dream, seven ears of corn came up on one stalk. These were good healthy looking corn. Another seven ears of corn sprang up but these were thin and unhealthy looking corn. The strange thing about his dream was that the seven thin ears of corn swallowed up the seven big ears of corn.

Pharaoh was confused. The next morning he called for all of his people who made up his own personal psychic network, but they were unable to help him. Then the chief butler told Pharaoh about a man named Joseph whom he remembered from time he spent with him in prison. He explained that Joseph had the ability to interpret dreams. Pharaoh sent for Joseph and told him about his dreams. Joseph explained to Pharaoh that his dreams represented seven years of plenty and seven years of famine for Egypt. Joseph suggested that Pharaoh find a wise man, give him some co-workers and put him in charge of the entire land. Their job would be to collect a fifth of all the food that was grown during the seven good years and store it for the seven bad years.

Joseph was the only man that Pharaoh saw as qualified for the job. As a result, he went from being a prisoner, to being the man in charge of the well-being of the people of Egypt. Due to his wisdom, people throughout the entire land of Egypt and the surrounding areas survived the seven years of famine. (Genesis 41, paraphrased)

What about you? What kind of mind do you have? Is it a foolish mind or a wise mind? Are you making preparations for eternity or are you waiting until the time comes to deal with it then? If that is what you are doing, you have a foolish mind.

There is not one person on this earth who knows the exact time that they are going to die, yet we take our own sweet time in making our decision about where we are going to spend eternity. Is that a foolish mind or what? We don't know if we are going to be alive at the end of the day, yet we have the audacity to think that we are in control of our lives. We don't know what is going to happen in the next second, yet we make plans without even checking with God, who is in charge of everything.

We know that satan (the adversary or the one who opposes God) is a deceiver and wants nothing but evil for our lives, yet so many of us continue to say no to Christ and yes to satan.

You may disagree with me and say that you have never said yes to satan and you never will, but every time you live in disobedience to the word of God you are saying yes to satan and whatever is represented as being in opposition to God.

God did not create robots that serve Him on command. He created human beings who have free will and are able to decide for themselves whether or not they want to worship Him. He leaves the choice up to us as to whether or not we will spend eternity with Him.

Wherever you end up spending eternity will be the determining factor as to whether you have a foolish mind or a wise mind. Not only that—you will have forever to live with your findings and no one to congratulate or blame but yourself.

REVIEW

1) What was Pharaoh's first dream about?

_____
_____
_____
_____

2) What was Pharaoh's second dream about?

_____
_____
_____

3) Were Pharaoh's psychics able to interpret his dreams for him?

_____

4) Who was the only one able to interpret Pharaoh's dreams?

_____

5) Explain the interpretation of Pharaoh's dream.

_____
_____
_____
_____
_____
_____
_____
_____

6) What was Joseph's reward for being able to interpret Pharaoh's dream?

_____

_____

_____

_____

7) In Matthew 16:23, Jesus referred to Peter as satan. Define the word satan as explained in this lesson and in the scripture verse above.

_____

_____

_____

_____

8) What will be the determining factor as to whether or not you have a foolish mind or a wise mind?

_____

_____

_____

_____

Chapter Six

A COMMITTED MIND

A PERSON WITH A committed mind is a person whose mind is at peace and the person whose mind is at peace is a person whose trust is in God.

Isaiah 26:3 says,

Thou wilt keep him in perfect peace, whose mind is stayed on thee.

Shadrach, Meshach and Abednego

Shadrach, Meshach and Abednego were three Hebrew boys who were brought to Babylon, along with Daniel, during the reign of King Nebuchadnezzar. They were a part of the group selected to serve in the King's palace.

These young men had a very strict diet that was the complete opposite of the diet that they were now being introduced to. Due to their strong faith and commitment to God, they would not eat the food that the King expected them to eat because it would defile their bodies. They made a request of the person in charge of their well-being, to allow them to stay on a vegetarian diet with water for ten days, then compare them with the others and see who was in better shape. He agreed and at the end of the ten days, they looked healthier and better nourished than all of the other men who ate the food supplied by the King. Needless to say, he let them stay on their own diet. (Daniel 1, Paraphrased)

King Nebuchadnezzar made a golden statue that was ninety feet high and nine feet wide and put it where everyone could see it. Whenever the music was played, everyone was supposed to stop whatever it was they were doing, fall down and worship the golden statue. Whoever didn't worship the statue would be thrown into a fiery furnace. Shadrach, Meshach and Abednego served only one God—the God of Abraham, Isaac and Jacob—and they were not about to worship any other god.

This was told to Nebuchadnezzar and he was furious. He sent for these three Hebrew boys and asked them why they weren't obeying his order to worship the golden statue. They told him that they didn't need to defend what they were doing because even if they were thrown into the furnace, God could deliver them from the furnace and from under his power. More than that, even if God chose not to deliver them they would never bow down and worship his statue. (Daniel 3)

They were so confident in their relationship with God that they had no fear of what would happen to their physical bodies. They were at peace even in that drastic situation because their minds were always on God and the things of God.

I am certain that there were other Hebrew people who bowed instead of standing tall for God, but Shadrach Meshach and Abednego decided that they were going to take a stand for righteousness. They could have done the "right thing" like some of their people, by doing what was necessary to save their lives. They could have eaten the food, bowed down to the statute and then prayed for forgiveness, but they chose to be obedient to God.

Their commitment to God led them to study all the things of God. This studying of the things of God led to their understanding of the absolute power of God, which led to their understanding of God's total control in every situation in their lives. This understanding of God's total control over every situation in their lives led to a faith in

God that could not be shaken—a faith that led to a peace that passes all understanding. This peace led to the acceptance that whatever God allows in the lives of those who believe on Him and trust in Him—whether good or bad—will work out for their good.

Romans 8:28 says,

And we know that all things work together for good to them that love God, to them who are the called, according to His purpose

This peace—this indescribable peace—only served to strengthen Shadrach, Meshach and Abednego's faith in God when they were faced with a life-threatening situation.

We as children of the same God, must seek and pursue this peace (1Peter 3: 11b) so that when we are faced with our own fiery furnace of trials, we too can stand assured that we will not do what is right according to man and save ourselves but we will do what is right according to God and save our souls.

REVIEW

1) Explain the characteristics of a person with a committed mind.

_____

_____

_____

_____

_____

_____

_____

_____

2) When were Daniel, Shadrach, Meshach and Abednego brought to Babylon?

_____

_____

_____

_____

3) How did they show their strong faith and commitment to God?

_____

_____

_____

4) What did King Nebuchadnezzar create and what did he expect the people to do whenever the music was played?

_____

_____

_____

_____

5) What would happen o anyone who disobeyed his command?

_____

_____

6) Who refused to obey Nebuchadnezzar's order and what was their statement of faith?

_____

_____

_____

_____

7) What was the result of their commitment to God?

_____

_____

8) Write Romans 8:28

_____

_____

_____

_____

_____

_____

_____

_____

Chapter Seven

THE CARNAL MIND

CCORDING TO WEBSTER'S dictionary, the word carnal means:

1. In and of the flesh; material or worldly, not spiritual.
2. Sensual; sexual

In Romans 8: 6-8 we get a very clear description of the carnal mind.

1. It is described as a mind concerned with the things of the flesh.
2. To be carnally minded is death
3. The carnal mind is at enmity with God.
4. The carnal mind cannot please God.

Can a person be saved and be carnally minded? Yes. When you accept the Lord Jesus Christ as your personal Savior, this is the first step in the cleansing process known as renewing the mind. All that you were before you accepted Jesus Christ into your life—your thoughts, your actions, your beliefs—are very much a part of who you are. They must now be changed and adapted to your new lifestyle, which is now under the direction of God.

In order for this to take place, you need to spend a lot of time in the Word, learning all you can about God and what He expects of us as

His children. Once you understand what the Bible is saying to you, you must begin to put it into practise. That is how the changes take place in your life—your mind begins the renewal process—and you go from being carnally minded to being spiritually minded.

Signs of a Carnal Mind

Keep in mind that the carnal mind is a mind that is concerned with the things of the flesh.

Galatians 5:19-21

19) Now the works of the flesh are manifest, which are these; adultery, fornication, uncleanness, lasciviousness,
20) Idolatry, witchcraft, hatred, variance, emulations, wrath, strife, seditions, heresies,
21) Envyings, murders, drunkenness, revellings, and such like: of the which I tell you before, as I have told you in time past, that they which do such things shall not inherit the kingdom of God.

Whatever you work at is what you practise and what you practise becomes perfect (routine) and obvious to those around you.

Each aspect of the works of the flesh would become null and void if there were no active participants to practise them and give them life. Why? They all need a human being to activate them and express them in order for them to exist.

Would there be such a thing as adultery or fornication if no two persons in the entire world practised them? What about witchcraft? Do you think that it would be such a financially rewarding business if instead of seeking psychics to guide them into the future, people accepted Jesus as their personal Savior and allowed the Holy Spirit to guide them in all things?

If people chose to love rather than hate and live in peace with each other rather than strive against each other, can you even begin to imagine how different this world would be?

The list can go on and on, but the simple fact of the matter is that it takes people to give life to the works of the flesh and we, as children of God, have to make a conscious choice not to support the flesh in any way. We must practise doing the opposite of what the works of the flesh wants us to do by practicing the things that God wants us to do.

A lot of us have read this passage of scripture (Galatians 5:19-21) over and over again and never took the time to get a full understanding of the characteristics of the works of the flesh. It is not surprising then, that it is this aspect of our walk with God that gives us the most trouble.

Some of us don't even know what some of those words listed as works of the flesh mean. That's probably why we live defeated Christian lives in the flesh instead of victorious lives in the spirit.

Learn the meanings of these words; meditate upon them and whenever satan tries to get you to actively participate in any of these activities, just remember that you want no part in helping him to build or strengthen his kingdom in any way and choose not to practise them. (All definitions are from Webster's dictionary unless otherwise indicated).

Adultery
Sexual intercourse between a man and a woman not his wife, or between a married woman and a man not her husband

Fornication
Sexual intercourse between an unmarried man and an unmarried woman.

Uncleanness
Unlawful sexual practices i.e. Homosexuality, lesbianism

Lasciviousness
1. Characterized by or expressing lust or lewdness; wanton.
2. Tending to excite lustful desires

Idolatry
The worship of idols, images, etc. (you can also idolize a person when your admiration of them turns to adoration)

Witchcraft
Witchcraft (divination) is a foretelling of future events, or discovering things secret by the aid of superior beings or other than human means. It is used in scripture of false systems of ascertaining the divine will (of God) (Smith's Bible Dictionary)

Hatred
Hate—to dislike greatly

Variance
Tendency to change (can't make up your mind)

Emulations
From the word emulate which means to strive to equal or excel. Emulations is defined as ambitious rivalry.

Wrath
Violent anger

Strife
Contention with another

Envyings
Feelings of discontent and ill will because of another's advantages or possessions

Murders
Murder is not limited to the physical killing of another human being as it also involves the destruction of one's character through malicious gossip (personal)

Drunkenness
A condition of being drunk

Revellings
Revel—To make merry; to be noisily festive (life is one big party)

REVIEW

1) Define the word carnal.

_____

_____

_____

_____

2) Describe the carnal mind as explained in Romans 8: 6-8

_____

_____

_____

_____

_____

_____

_____

3) Explain the process of moving from a carnal mind to a spiritual mind.

_____

_____

_____

_____

_____

_____

_____

_____

4) What are the signs of a carnal mind or the works of the flesh, as listed in Galatians 5: 19-21?

_____

_____

_____

_____

_____

_____

_____

_____

Chapter Eight

THE MIND OF THE SPIRIT

I F YOU HAVE accepted Jesus Christ as your personal Savior and the fruit of the Spirit is not evident in your life, you need to have your mind renewed through the Word of God and start practicing what the Word of God says you should be doing.

Just how we have to be active participants in the works of the flesh in order for them to have a negative impact in our lives and the lives of those with whom we come in contact, we must also be active participants in the development of the fruit of the Spirit in our lives, in order for them to be effective in us and in the lives of others with whom we come in contact.

Active participation in the development of the fruit of the Spirit results in the death of the works of the flesh. Where love is being preached, hatred cannot survive; where peace is being practised, there can be no wrath or strife and where faith in God is being practised, there is no need to practise witchcraft.

It is not easy developing the fruit of the Spirit in your life because it is not something that automatically appears when you get saved. You have to actually choose to love rather than hate, especially when someone has hurt you and in some cases has never apologized or asked for your forgiveness.

There will be times when things will not be going well with you and you may want to wallow in your sorrows, but in the midst of it all, you must practice joy and happiness in the Lord.

To put it in a nutshell, the opposite of having a carnal mind is having a mind that is controlled by the Spirit of God and a mind that is controlled by the Spirit of God will result in the fruit of the Spirit being evident in a person's life.

What are the fruit of the Spirit? We find the answer in Galatians 5:22-23.

> 22) But the fruit of the Spirit is love, joy, peace,
> longsuffering, gentleness, goodness, faith,
> 23) Meekness, temperance . . . .

Sometimes difficulties will arise and it will feel like they are taking forever to be resolved, but in the midst of it all, you must be longsuffering—exercise patience—knowing that God is working everything out in His way, in His time and for your good.

Sometimes something or someone will put us in a position that really gets us upset but it is at this time that we must practice temperance, because our reaction could either be a witness for God or a witness against God.

The only way that we can destroy the works of the flesh is through the development of the fruit of the Spirit—the key being not retaliating in the flesh but participating in the Spirit.

Learn the meanings of these words and make them a part of your daily walk with God.

Love
A strong affection for or attachment or devotion to a person or persons

Joy
A very glad feeling, happiness

Peace
Freedom from disagreements or quarrels, an undisturbed state of mind; absence of mental conflict; calm; quiet; tranquility

Longsuffering
Patience, not easily provoked

Gentleness
Mildness, tenderness, softness

Goodness
The state or quality of being good; kindness; generosity

Faith
Unquestioning belief in God

Meekness
Meek—patient and mild; not inclined to anger or resentment

Temperance
Self control in conduct, expression, indulgence of the appetite etc . . .

We are what we choose to become and we become what we practice.

Destroy the works of the flesh in your life by actively participating in the development of the fruit of the Spirit in your life.

REVIEW

1) What is the opposite of having a carnal mind?

_____

_____

_____

_____

2) What do we have to do in order for the fruit of the Spirit to be developed in our lives?

_____

_____

_____

_____

3) What is the result of a mind controlled by the Spirit of God?

_____

_____

4) In your own words, express your understanding of the fruit of the Spirit.

_____

_____

_____

_____

_____

_____

_____

_____

_____

_____

_____

_____

If you would like to contact the author,
please send your questions or comments to:

Velyn Cooper
P. O. Box F42524
Freeport, Grand Bahama
Bahamas

email: biblicaljourneys@gmail.com

website: http://biblicaljourneys.weebly.com